T0069337

curious creatures

stickers and activities

curious creatures

stickers and activities

Anita Ganeri and Penny Arlon

weldonowen

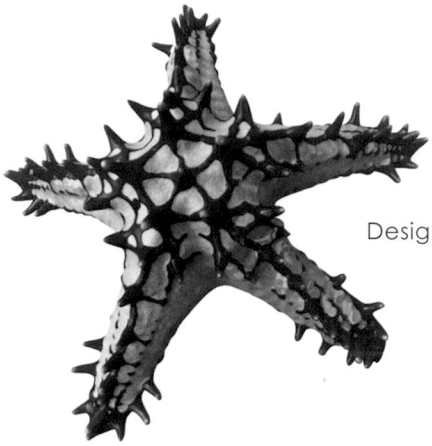

weldon**owen**

Authors: Anita Ganeri and Penny Arlon

Design: Tory Gordon-Harris, Peter Clayman, Anna Pond

Editorial: Lydia Halliday, Susie Rae

Fact checker: Jenny Curran

Art Director: Stuart Smith

Publisher: Sue Grabham

Insight Editions Publisher: Raoul Goff

All photographs in this book including those used on the cover are used under license from Shutterstock.com

Copyright © Weldon Owen International, L.P. 2021

All rights reserved. No part of this publication may be reproduced, distributed, or transmitted in any form or by any means, including photocopying, recording, or other electronic or mechanical methods, without the prior written permission of the publisher, except in the case of brief quotations embodied in critical reviews and certain other noncommercial uses permitted by copyright law.

Published by Weldon Owen Children's Books

An imprint of Weldon Owen International, L.P.

A subsidiary of Insight International, L.P.

PO Box 3088
San Rafael, CA 94912

www.insighteditions.com

ISBN: 978-1-68188-741-8

Manufactured in China

First printed in 2020

23 22 21 20 19 1 2 3 4 5

Contents

Eyes and ears	8
Fur, feather, and prickles	18
Patterns	28
Beaks, bills, and noses	36
Shells and scales	46
Tusks, horns, and antlers	54
Tails	62
Body shapes	70
Arms, legs, hands, and feet	78
Wings	86
Teeth and claws	94
Glow in the dark	104

Look for the fun activities in each chapter. There are mazes, dot to dots, word searches, sticker scenes, and more!

Find the giant poster and sticker sheets at the end of the book!

Curious Creatures

Some creatures have big ears, long noses, or huge eyes. Some have amazing shells and scales. Others are covered in hair, feathers, scales, or prickles. Some creatures have oddly shaped bodies, with incredible colors and patterns. Others have the astonishing ability to glow in the dark. There are millions of curious creatures on planet Earth, and billions of different creature features and shapes. A creature's appearance isn't simply for show, though—it is much more important than that. In the natural world, an animal's body shape has evolved over millions of years, and helps an animal to survive wherever it lives.

Some features, such as long arms, wings, or flippers, allow animals to move on land, water, and air. Orangutans use their extra-long arms to swing through the trees in their forest home. Birds use their wings for flying, while fish have fins and tails for swimming. Colors and patterns help animals to stay hidden, so that their enemies cannot see them, or they can sneak up on prey. They can also be a way for animals to send signals and keep in touch. Many features help animals to track down and eat their food. Animals that eat meat have sharp teeth and claws. Birds have bills and beaks specially adapted for eating leaves, fruit, and seeds, and for cracking nuts. Eyes, ears, and noses are essential sense organs for finding food in different places, and even in the dark.

In this book, you will meet a huge variety of curious creatures, from prickly porcupines and glittering glow-worms to sharp-toothed tigers and sea dragons shaped like seaweed. See if you can work out how their special features help them to stay alive.

Eyes and ears

Many animals rely on their senses of sight and hearing to find food and stay out of danger. Owls have huge eyes for hunting, particularly at night, and flexible necks that they can twist right around to look behind them. This owl's ears are on the sides of its head, covered by feathers. One ear is slightly higher than the other. The owl turns and tilts its head until it can hear equally in both ears. Then it can pinpoint the exact location of its prey.

Snail
Fly
Tokay gecko
Red piranha
Rabbit
Mottled garlic toad
Spider
Chinchilla
Koala
Crested gecko
Chicken
Lovebird
Sphynx cat
Donkey
Frog
Hen harrier
Yellow eyelash viper
Caracal
Ostrich
Garden dormouse

Gecko
Dragonfly
Rabbit
Mandarin duck
Bull terrier
Mouse
Flying fox
Snail
Lynx
Red squirrel
European scops owls
Jackson's chameleon
Hammerhead shark
Tiger
Beagle
Persian cat
Northern white-faced owl
European otter
Red-eyed tree frog

Fly
Australian shepherd
Blue-eye rainbow fish
Giraffe
Maine coon
Snowflake moray
Crowned sifaka
Domestic Pig
Dwarf neon rainbowfish
Caique parrot
Argentine horned frog
Common seal pup
Tree frogs
French bulldog
Red panda
Eagle owl
Friesian cow

Senegal bushbaby
Longhorn cowfish
Russian rabbit
White rabbit
Green aracari
Shrimp
Hippopotamus
African elephant
Border collie
Telescope eye goldfish
Indian rhinoceros
Praying mantis
Brown bear
White tiger
Giant pandas

Eye spy

Keep an eye on these animal puzzles.
They are watching you from all directions!

Follow the lines

The hammerhead shark uses its wide eyes to find the squid. Which path should it take?

Hammerhead shark

Seaweed

Squid

Seaweed

EYES EVERYWHERE

The chameleon can roll its eyes up, down, backward, and forward. It can even move its eyes in different directions!

Sticker scene

How many red-eyed tree frogs can you find on your sticker sheet? Fill the forest with frogs!

Use your stickers here!

Maze

Can you help the eight-eyed spider through the maze?

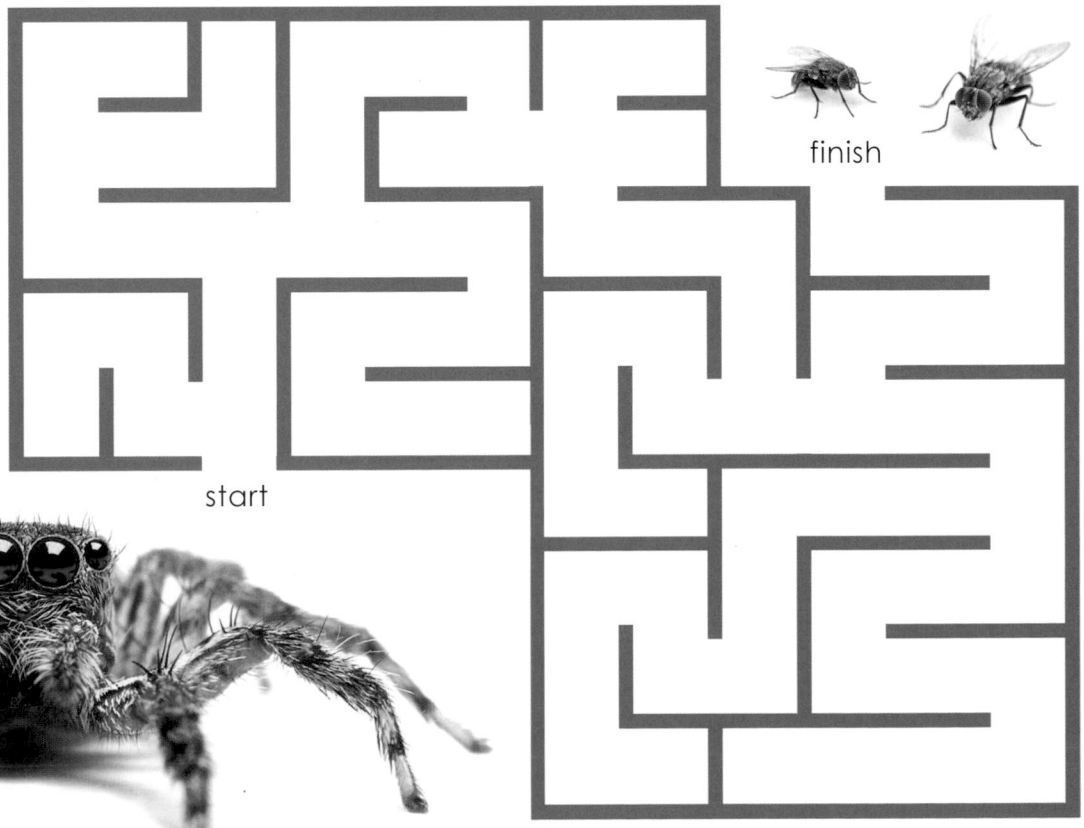

All ears

Animals with big ears have excellent hearing. Check out all the long, wide, floppy, and flappy ears in these puzzles!

Matching pair

Can you find the two identical fennec fox cubs?

NIGHT EARS

This brown long-eared bat has huge ears! It can hear very well. Bats have the best hearing of any land animal, but not good eyesight.

Dot to dot

Connect the dots, starting with number 1.
Find the animal with the biggest ears of all!

Word search

These big-eared animals are all in this word grid. Can you find them?

s	d	f	k	c
m	o	o	s	e
c	g	c	w	l
o	h	a	r	e
w	e	t	w	v

Cow

Dog

Hare

Cat

Moose

Fur, feathers, and prickles

A fur coat can be vital for keeping an animal warm, and creatures that live in the coldest places often have the longest and thickest fur. Feathers do a similar job, and also help birds to fly. Fur and feathers can be waterproof, but need to be kept in top condition. Some creatures, like this porcupine, are covered in thousands of needle-like prickles or quills, made from sharp, hard hairs. The quills lie flat, until the porcupine is threatened. Then they shoot up, ready to launch a painful defense.

Chinchilla
Hedgehogs
Irish cob horse
Thorny devil lizard
Hooded pitta
Bactrian camel
Rabbit
Roosters
Echidna
Chicks
Guinea pig
Caterpillar
Angora rabbit
Macaw
Ducklings

Lionfish
Bee
Barn owl
Porcupines
German spitz
Lovebirds
Bullfinch
Zebra finch
Alpaca
Echidna
Wild goose
Sheep
Ferret
Giant prickly stick insect
Knob-tailed gecko
Pufferfish
Armadillo lizard

Rainbow lorikeet
Pied kingfisher
Mountain goat
Coypu
Brown bear cub
Llama
Japanese cranes
Andean bear
Highland cow
Shetland pony
Draft horse
Buffalo
Cockatoo
Raccoon
Swallow
Bactrian camel
Snow monkeys
Brown bear

Afghan hound
Gray heron
Hill blue flycatcher
Kalij pheasants
Caterpillar
Wolves
Lion
Baby orangutan
Polar bear
Bee-eater
Buck moth caterpillar
Macaw
Ornamental fish
Bald eagle
Rhesus monkey
Arctic fox
Husky
Mountain goat
Shih-tzu

Fur and prickles

Some animals are furry and others are spiny. Can you find an animal that is furry and spiny?

Shadow hunt

The furry animals are looking for their shadows. Which shadow is missing?

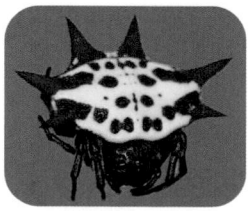

SPINY SHOCK

When the puffer fish is attacked, it doesn't swim away. It blows its body up like a balloon and sticks out its prickles. Nothing will eat that!

Sticker scene

Use your sticker sheet to find the prickly hedgehogs. Add them to their forest home.

Use your stickers here!

How many left?

The furry, spiny caterpillars are hungry. Are there enough leaves for all of the caterpillars?

Feathers

Look at all the birds in these feathery puzzles! Birds are the only animals in the world that have feathers.

Spot the difference

Can you spot two differences between these two stunning peacocks?

FEATHERY WARM

Emperor penguins live in very cold places. They have thousands of waterproof feathers that keep them toasty warm in the snow.

What comes next?

Look at the animals below and work out which bird comes next on each line.

Use your stickers here!

Matching pair

Can you spot two feathers that are the exactly the same?

Color me in

Parrots have lots of different colored feathers. How many colors will yours have?

Patterns

The patterned coats of some creatures help them to blend into the background, hide from hungry enemies, or lie in wait, unseen, for prey. Some animals, such as chameleons and cuttlefish, can even change color to show their feelings and communicate. These zebras' striking black-and-white coats would seem to make them stand out in a crowd. In fact, their stunning stripes are useful for confusing predators who find it tricky to pick out a single zebra from among the others in the herd.

Wasp
Hornet
Sailfin fish
Pearl stingray
Budgerigar
Gecko
Clownfish
Giraffe
Blue poison dart frogs
Butterflies
Tiger
Malayan banded pitta
California quail
Wood beetle

Quoll
Mandarin duck
Snowy owl
Reed frog
Leopard frog
Starling
Asian leopard cat
Triggerfish
Cheetah
Blue-tongued lizard
Fresian cow
European turtle dove
Ocellated lizard
Harlequin frogs
Royal angelfish
Baby tapir
Royal pheasant
Lynx
Cobra
Lantern bug

Ladybug
Zebras
Fire salamander
Common pheasant
Painted lady butterfly
Asian leopard cat
Orcas
Jaguars
Dalmatian
Bengal cat
Okapi
Waxwing
Panther chameleon

Jewel beetles
Flap-necked chameleon
Whale Shark
Sea turtle
Leopards
Pueblan milk snake
Bumblebee
White tiger
Fresh spotted scat fish
Neon tetra fish
Alligator bug
Bumblebee goby
Butterfly tiger moth
Lambs
Gray peacock-pheasant
Great mormon butterflies

Patterns

The animal world is filled with spots, stripes, and other colorful markings. Which pattern is your favorite?

Word search

Can you find these patterned creatures in the word grid?

d	m	p	t	f
u	k	t	i	i
c	d	v	g	s
k	b	e	e	h
z	e	b	r	a

Bee

Fish

Zebra

Duck

Tiger

EYE SPOTS

When the sunbittern bird is afraid, it opens its wings. The patterns look like huge eyes and scare other animals away!

Help the giraffe

The giraffe wants to get to the acacia leaf. Can you help?

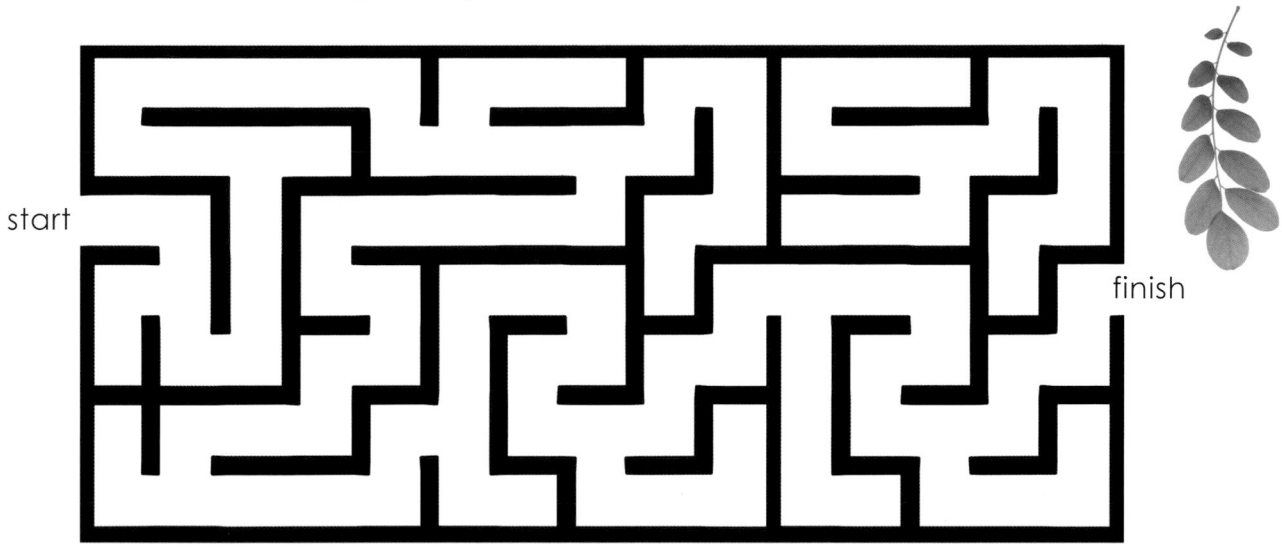

Odd one out

Look carefully at the snakes. Which one doesn't match the others?

Draw the other half

Can you copy the patterns on the other side of the butterfly?

Beaks, bills, and noses

A bird's beak or bill has many functions—finding food, preening feathers, and feeding young, to name just a few. Beaks and bills vary in shape depending on what the bird eats. An oystercatcher uses its long, thin bill for probing mud for shellfish. A macaw cracks nuts with its strong, hooked beak. And noses aren't just for smelling either. This male proboscis monkey uses its very large, fleshy nose to attract a mate and warn off rivals. Its nose helps to make its honking call louder and more impressive.

Common kingfisher
Blue marlin
Toco toucan
Hornbill
Tapir
Tree pit viper
Green mamba snake
Sandhill crane
Giant anteaters
Sulawesi hornbill
Spectacled caiman
Rat
Jack Russell
Chameleon
Koala
Emperor penguin

Hedgehog
South American coati
Nose horned viper
Quoll
Southern ground hornbill
Cow
Hooded vulture
Giraffe
Hornbill
Emperor penguin
Needlefish
Rats
Masked lovebirds
Collared anteater
Aardvark
Longnose butterflyfish
Mandrill
Rhinoceros beetle
Walrus
Red palm weevil
Pigeon
Hummingbird
Guinea pig

Bay horse
Spotted hyena
Rooster
Dusky hognose snake
Flamingos
Wild boar
Argentine red tegu
Northern caiman lizard
Sea lions
Tapir
Ferret
Vipera latastei snake
Hound dog
Syrian hamsters
Duckling
King vulture
Hoopoe
Koala
Gambian pouched rat

Fox
Sturgeon fish
Pigeon
Otters
Pig-nosed turtles
Pigs
Asian elephant
Hippopotamus
Malayan sunbear
Sea dolphin
Elephant
Proboscis monkey

Bird beaks

Bird beaks come in lots of shapes and sizes. Long beaks catch fish. Thick beaks can crack nuts. Can you see a curved beak?

Which one has most?

These puffins have been fishing. Which one has caught the most fish?

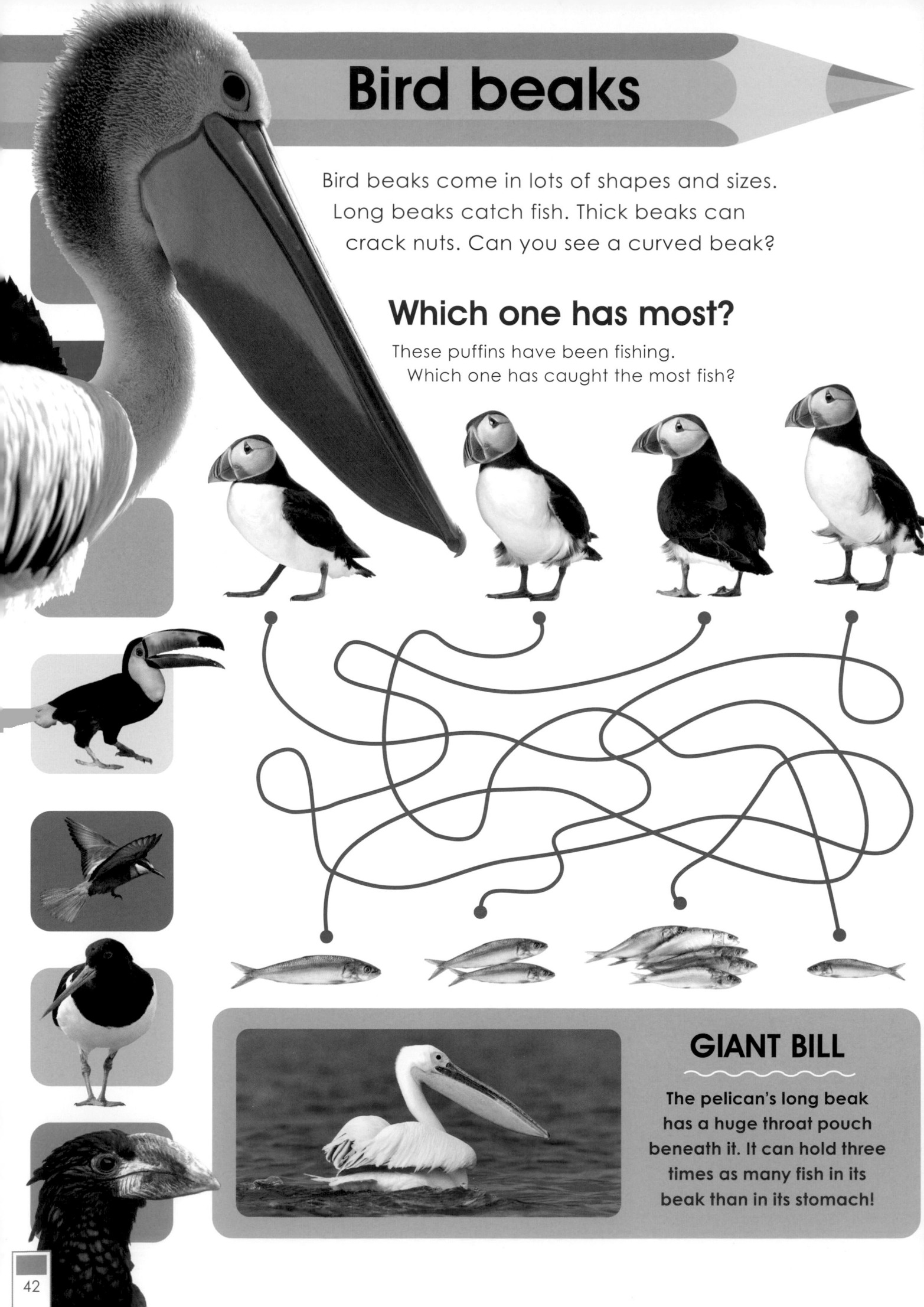

GIANT BILL

The pelican's long beak has a huge throat pouch beneath it. It can hold three times as many fish in its beak than in its stomach!

Find the shadows

Match the birds to their shadows. The beak shapes might help you.

Dot to dot

Connect the dots, starting at number 1. Can you find a bird with a beak as long as its body?

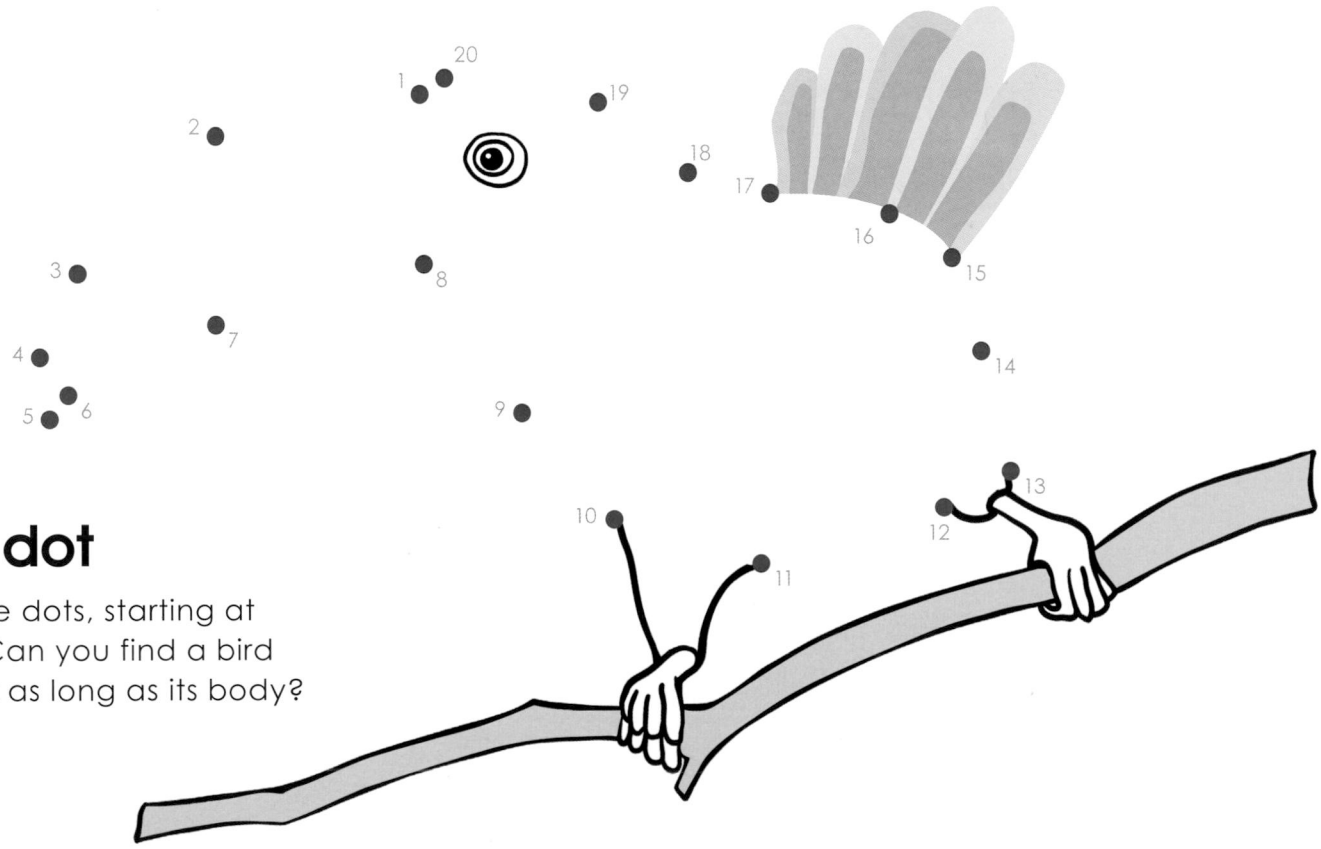

Noses

Get your nose stuck into these animal puzzles. Can you sniff out the answers?

Can you find?

The viper uses its nose to hunt animals. Can you help it find three birds, four lizards, and six mice?

SNIFF IT OUT

Great white sharks have an amazing sense of smell. They would be able to smell one drop of blood in a swimming pool!

Follow the nose

The anteater is following its nose to the anthill. Which line should it take?

Matching pair

Check out the mandrills' noses! Can you spot the matching pair?

Shells and scales

Some creatures grow scales and shells to protect their soft bodies. Crocodiles and lizards have larger scales around their heads, tails, and feet, and smaller scales around their joints. Other animals grow shells around them—think of the seashells you find on the beach. They are left behind by creatures, such as cockles, mussels, and clams. A sea turtle's shell is amazing. It is made from bone and cartilage. This leatherback turtle is slightly different—it has tough, leathery skin.

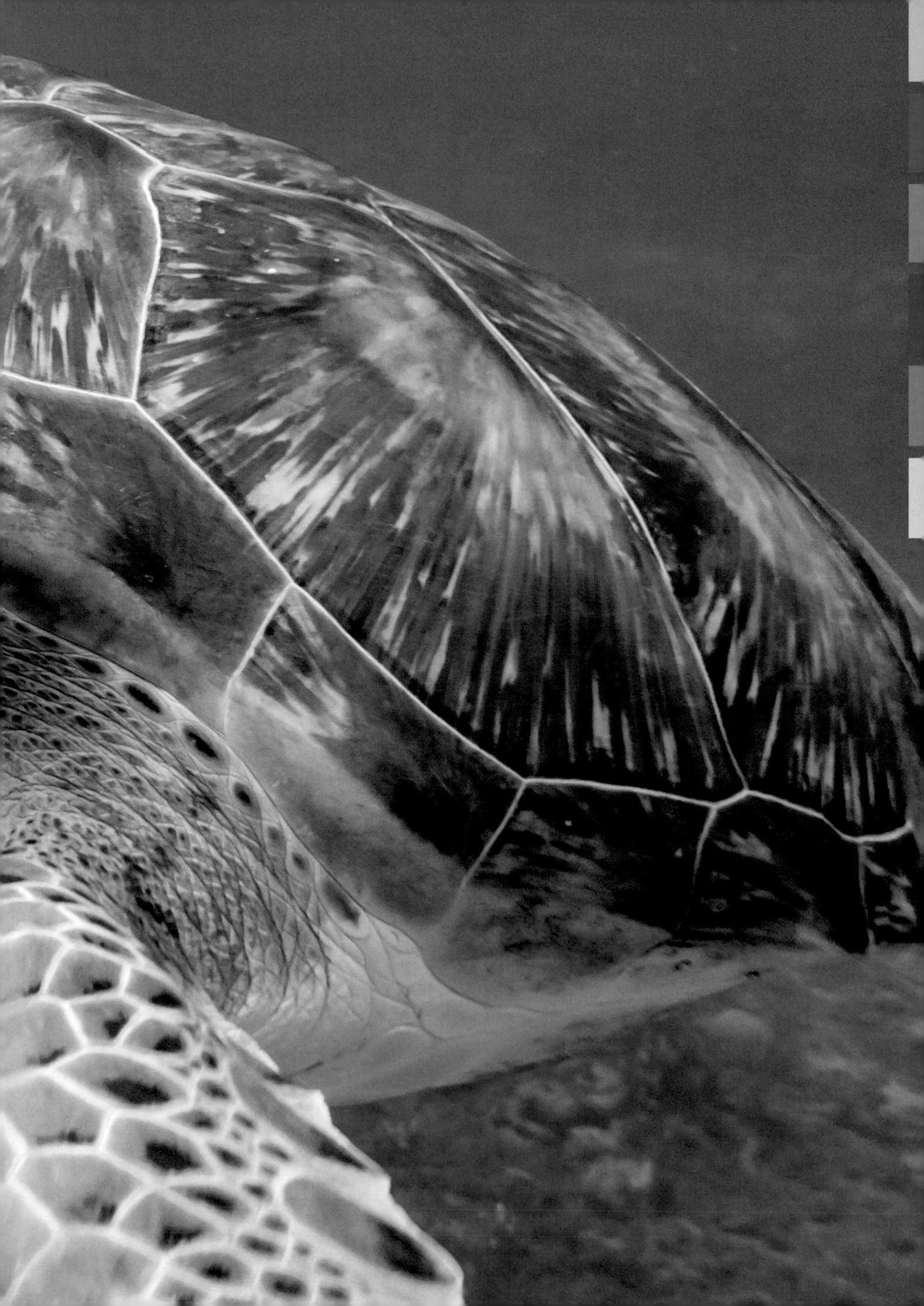

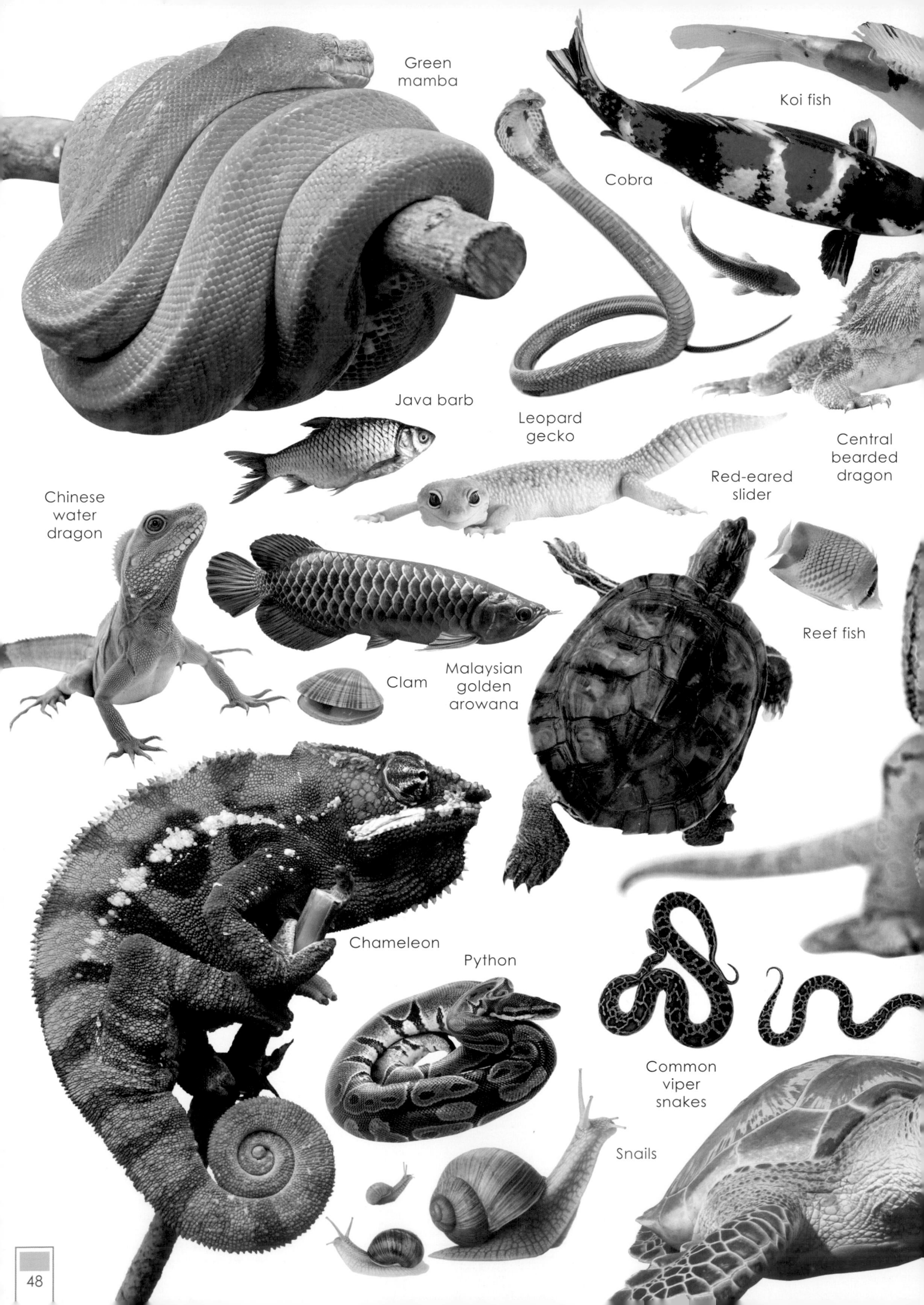
Green mamba
Koi fish
Cobra
Java barb
Leopard gecko
Central bearded dragon
Red-eared slider
Chinese water dragon
Reef fish
Clam
Malaysian golden arowana
Chameleon
Python
Common viper snakes
Snails

Field crab
Coahuilan box turtle
Iguana
Rainbow crab
African spurred tortoise
Freshwater crocodile
Freshwater prawn
Goldfish
Veiled chameleon
Tortoise
Tokay gecko
Hermit crab
Loggerhead turtles
Lobsters

Whelks
Lizard fish
Blue tongue skink
Australian freshwater crocodile
Viper
Mussels
Goldfish
Aldabra giant tortoises
Common adder
Gila monsters
Yabbie Crayfish
River Crayfish
New Caledonian crested geckos

Oyster
Leaf gecko
Red-eared slider
Garter snake
Caspian turtle
Fresh water crocodile
Green lizards
Sand lizard
Siamese fighting fish
Indian star tortoises
Corn snake
Iguana
Blue zaire frontosa
Giant sulcata tortoise
Grass snake

In a shell

When these animals feel scared, they hide in their shell homes. Which have come out of their shells?

Sticker scene

Can you find the turtle stickers on your sticker sheet? Put them on the reef.

Use your stickers here!

A SHELL HOME

The Galapagos tortoise is so big that a 10-year-old child could hide under its shell!

What comes next?

Can you work out which animal comes next on each line?

Use your stickers here!

Color me in

Use lots of bright colors to draw a swirly pattern on the snail's shell.

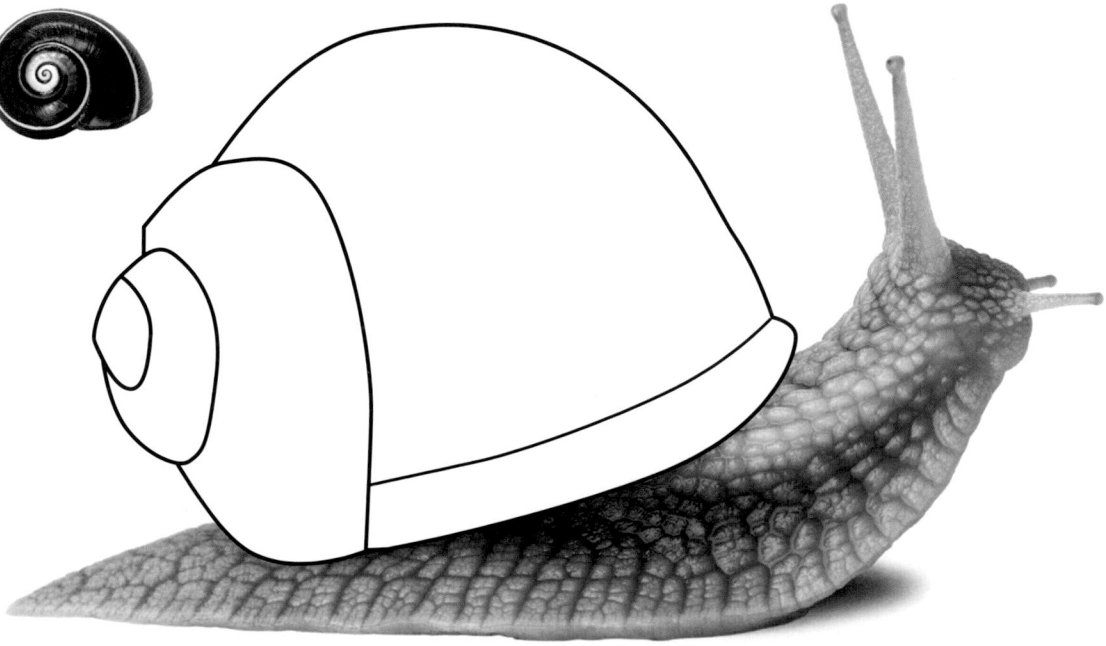

Odd one out

Only one shell does not have a matching twin. Can you find it?

Tusks, horns, and antlers

Tusks are front teeth that keep on growing, and they're found in wild boar, elephants, hippos, and walruses. A walrus's tremendous tusks can grow three feet long. They're used for breaking holes in the ice, and hauling their owner out of the water. They're also a status symbol—males with the largest tusks take the top spot in the herd. Horns are made from keratin like your hair and nails, and antlers are made from bone. They're grown by creatures, such as antelope, rhinos, and deer, for fighting rivals and defending territory.

Longhorn beetle
Moose
Red hartebeest
Jewel beetle
Cow
Yak
Surinam horned frog
Banteng
Wood-boring beetles
Wild boars
Goat
Bull elks
Mountain goats
Flower long-horn beetle
Pipevine swallowtail butterfly
Rocky mountain goat

Arles merino sheep
Waterbuck
Greater kudu
Big-horned beetles
Ankole-watusi
Sika deer
Red palm weevil
Longhorn beetle
Flower chafers
Red deer
Blackbucks
Rhinoceros beetle

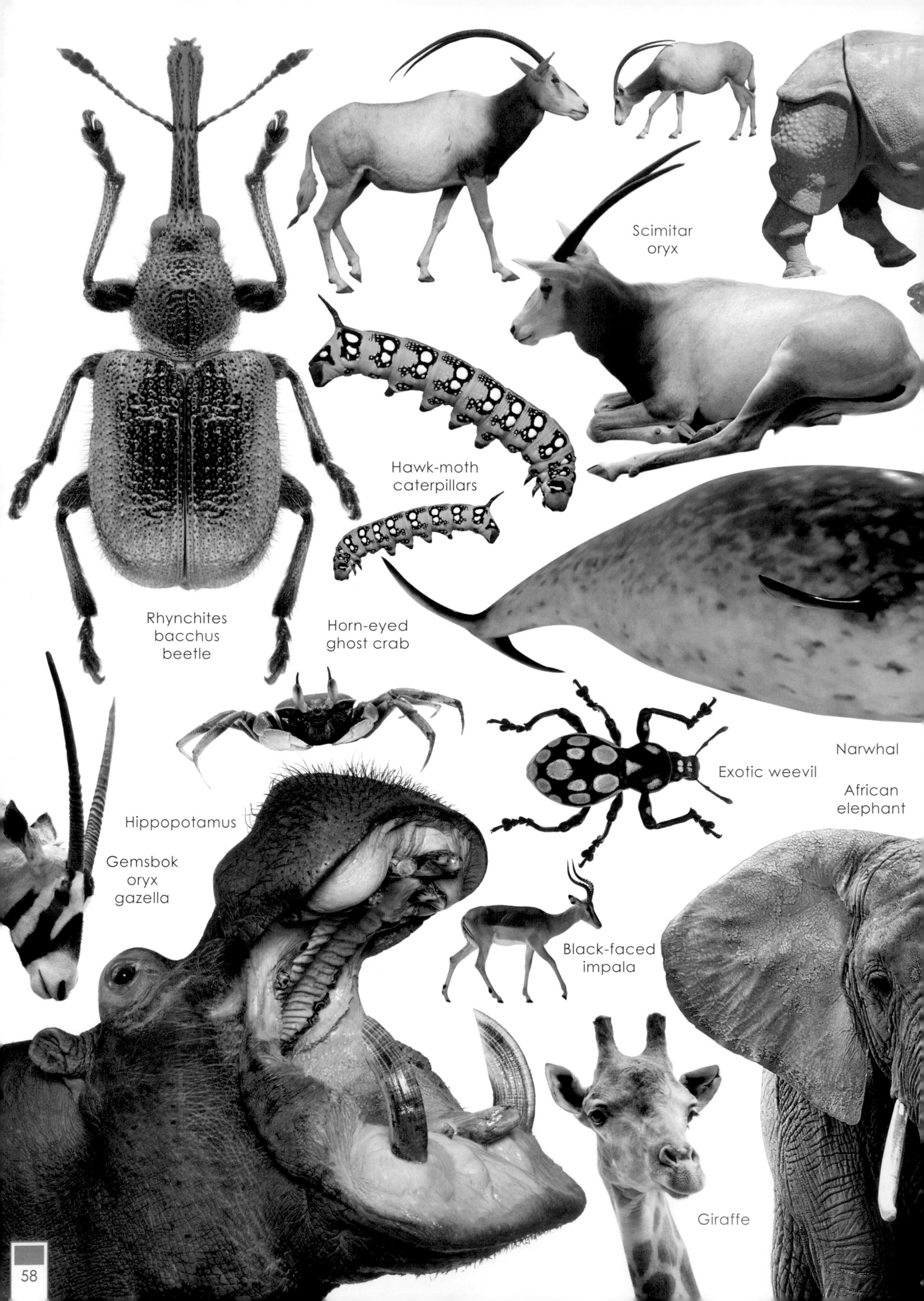
Scimitar oryx
Hawk-moth caterpillars
Rhynchites bacchus beetle
Horn-eyed ghost crab
Narwhal
Exotic weevil
African elephant
Hippopotamus
Gemsbok oryx gazella
Black-faced impala
Giraffe

Indian rhinoceros
Gaur
Namibian springbok
Black rhinoceros
Lanternflies
Asian elephant
Impala
Nyala
Desert horned lizard
Stag beetle
Asian elephants
Tropical beetle
Mouflon
Dorcas gazelle

Horns and antlers

Look for the horns, antlers, and tusks in these puzzles. Can you spot the animal with the curly horns?

Shadow search

Check out the animals' horns and antlers. Can you match the animals to their shadows?

NEW ANTLERS

The moose has huge antlers. Each winter the antlers drop off and new ones grow in the spring.

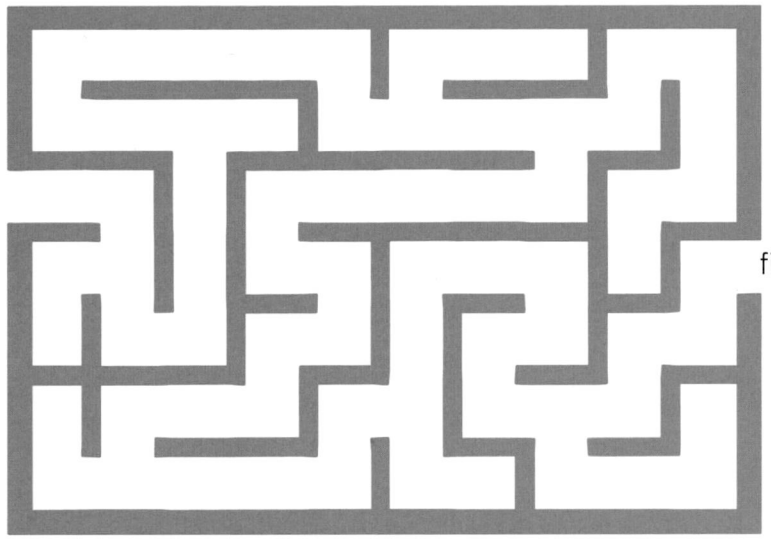

Maze

The long-toothed narwhal needs to find its way to the shrimp. Can you help it?

Word search

Find the animals with horns and tusks in the word grid.

r	s	g	t	f
h	b	o	a	r
i	f	a	n	o
n	l	t	z	g
o	k	u	d	u

Goat

Frog

Boar

Kudu

Rhino

Tails

As this whale dives, it lifts its tail high into the air, showing its two tail flukes. Underwater, it moves its tail and lower body up and down to power itself through the sea. Tails have many uses. They're used for brushing flies away, staying balanced, or gripping onto the branches of trees. Some animals, like dogs, show their feelings by the way in which they hold their tails. Ring-tailed lemurs walk through the forest, holding their striped tails high in the air. This helps to keep everyone in the group together.

Scorpion
Peacocks
Cat
South American coati
Macaws
Dolphin
Lizards
Gecko
Cottontail rabbit
Skunk
Earwig
Red kite
Cow
Ring-tailed lemur
Dachshund

Chameleon
Betta fish
Sugargliders
Orca
Flying lemur
Belgian heavy horse
Kangaroo
Zebra angelfish
Bay horse
Red fox
Egyptian jerboa
Guppies
Chameleon
Bell's dabb lizard
Siberian chipmunk
Armadillo
Pike

Pheasants
Barracuda
Blue tail skink
Rattlesnake
Red swordtail fish
Koi angelfish
Marlin
Himalayan bluetails
Turtle
Swallow-tailed kite
Kitten
Pig
Scarlet macaw
Squirrels
Elf cat
Ryukyu leaf turtle

Common marmoset
Sheep
Orange-breasted trogon
Shield-tailed agama
Crown tail fighting fish
Manta ray
Senegal bushbaby
Dwarf cichlids
Giant leaf tailed gecko
Green basilisk
Blue moon lobster
Western diamondback rattlesnakes
Lesser siren
Dusky leaf monkey
Sun conure parrot
Crocodile
Shark
Siberian sturgeon
Beaded lizards

Tail tasks

A tail is very useful. It can help with balance, swish away pests, and even grip onto branches. Which of these animals has the shortest tail?

Spot the difference

Can you spot two differences between these two flying parrots?

A NEW TAIL

If the green iguana loses its tail, a new one will grow back!

Find the bananas!

Spider monkeys uses their tails to swing from branch to branch. Which will reach the biggest bunch of bananas?

Draw the other half

How long can you make these vipers' tails? Draw them in and make them wiggly.

Body shapes

Curious creatures come in many different shapes. The shape of an animal's body tells you a lot about where and how it lives. Animals that live in the sea often have bodies that are streamlined for swimming. Animals that live underground are built for digging and wriggling through the soil. Some animals are shaped to look like their surroundings, for camouflage. This pygmy seahorse's bumpy, pink skin helps it to hide among its coral reef habitat.

Comet fish
Pygmy seahorse
Armadillos
Siamese fighting fish
Leaf insects
Moray eel
Sea star
Bird wrasse
Triggerfish
Pufferfish
Seahorse
Egyptian vulture
Ribbon eels

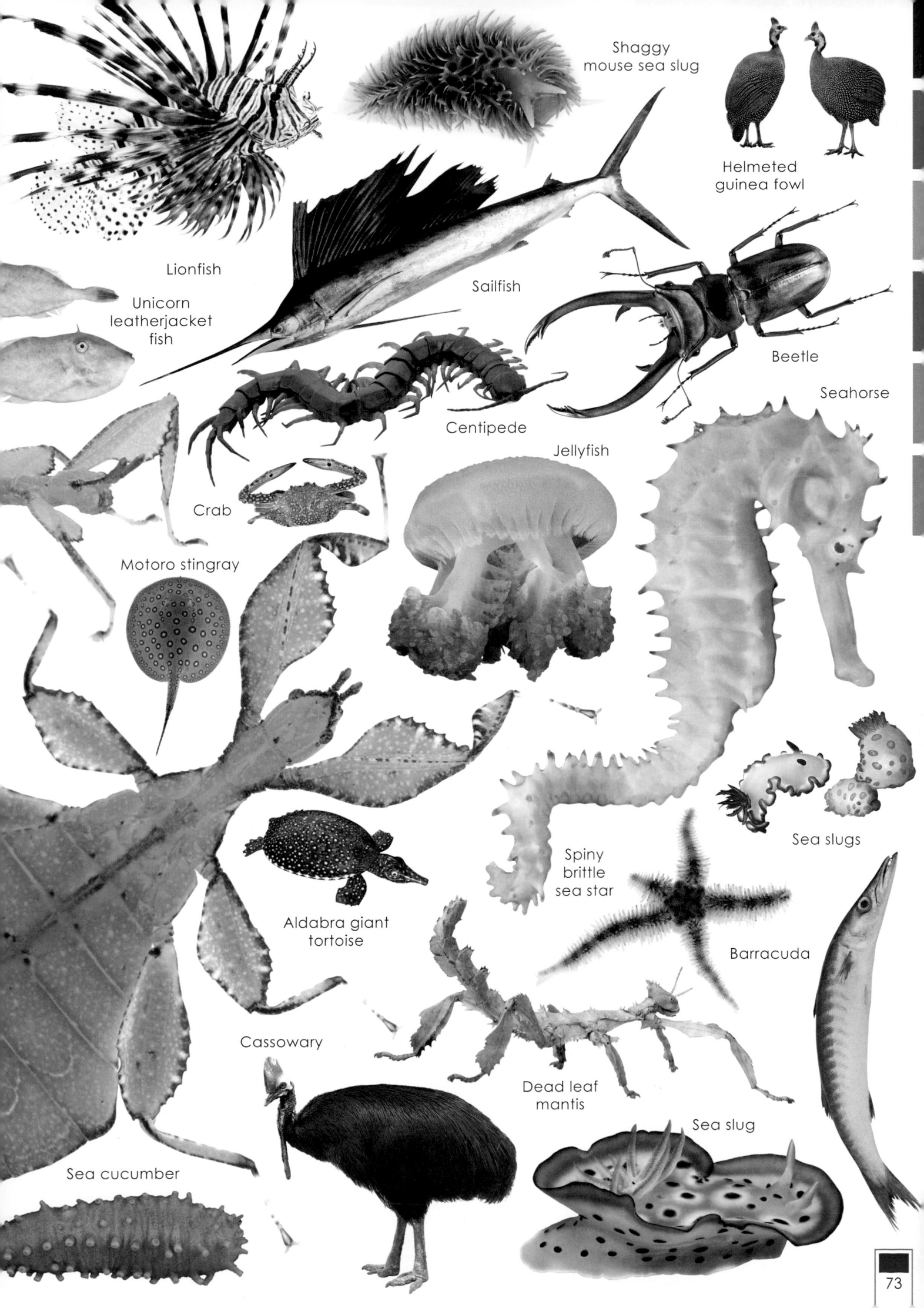
Shaggy mouse sea slug
Helmeted guinea fowl
Lionfish
Sailfish
Unicorn leatherjacket fish
Beetle
Seahorse
Centipede
Jellyfish
Crab
Motoro stingray
Sea slugs
Spiny brittle sea star
Aldabra giant tortoise
Barracuda
Cassowary
Dead leaf mantis
Sea slug
Sea cucumber

Flying lemur
Jellyfish
Octopuses
Leopard shark
Siamese fighting fish
Stingray
Shrimp
Saiga antelope
Echidna
Maned wolf
White whale
European mole
Lionfish
Discus fish

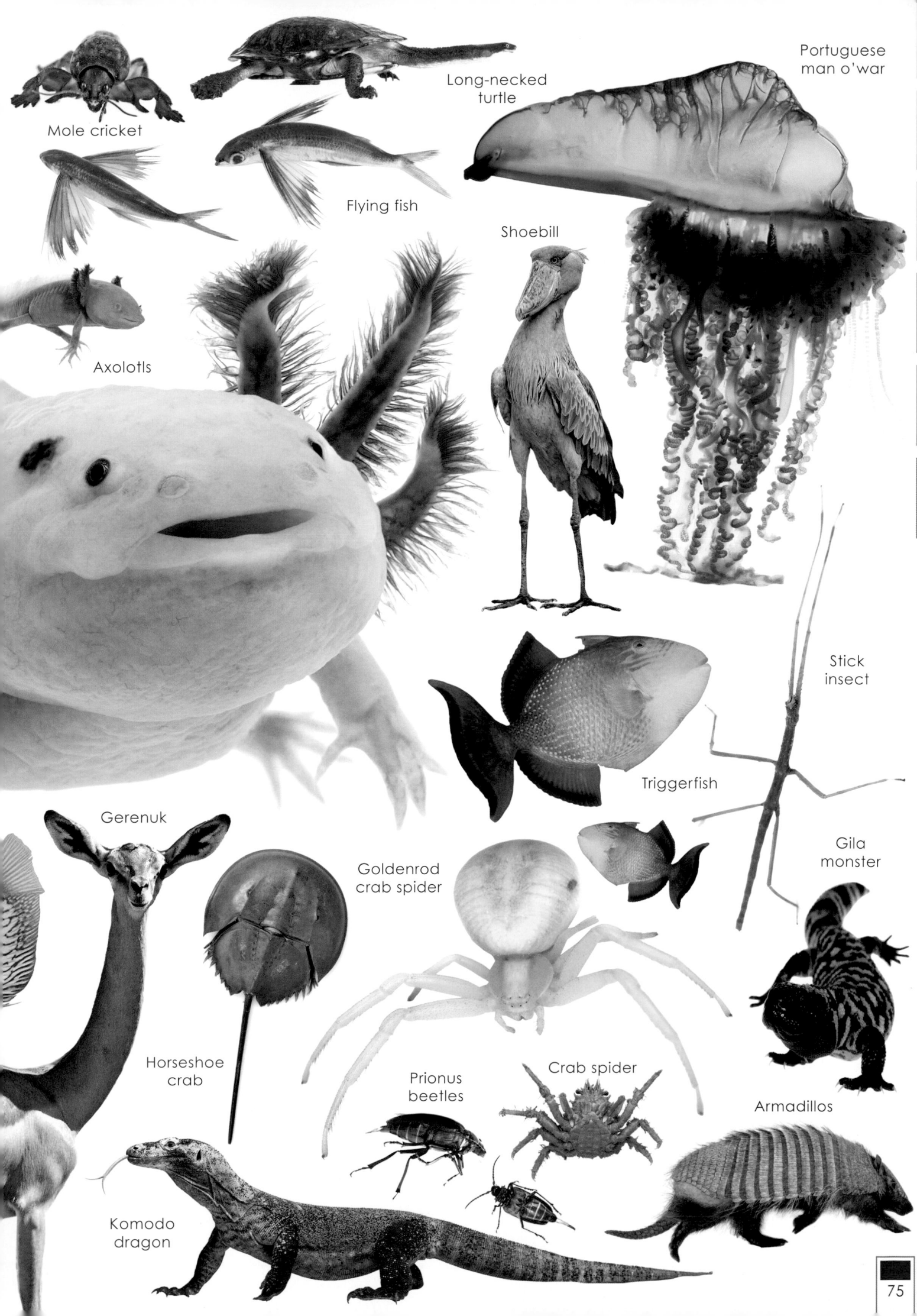
Mole cricket
Long-necked turtle
Portuguese man o'war
Flying fish
Shoebill
Axolotls
Stick insect
Triggerfish
Gerenuk
Gila monster
Goldenrod crab spider
Horseshoe crab
Crab spider
Prionus beetles
Armadillos
Komodo dragon

Shapes

There are some crazy shapes in the animal world. Look at all the different shapes of these creatures!

Find the shadows

Match the shadows to the strange-shaped creepy-crawlies.

Moon moth

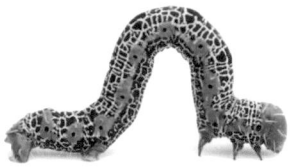

Caterpillar

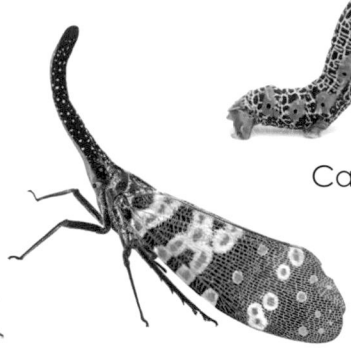

Lantern bug

Centipede

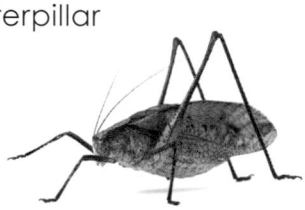

Katydid

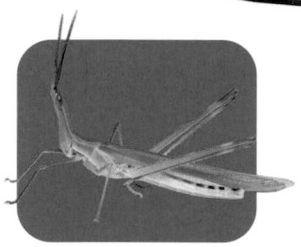

Odd one out

Which one of these curly pill millipedes doesn't have a matching twin?

IS IT A LEAF?

Leaf insects are the same shape as a leaf. If they need to hide, they just stay very still among green leaves!

How many left?

The spiky lionfish are looking for a piece of knobby coral to nibble. If there is one piece each, how many will go without?

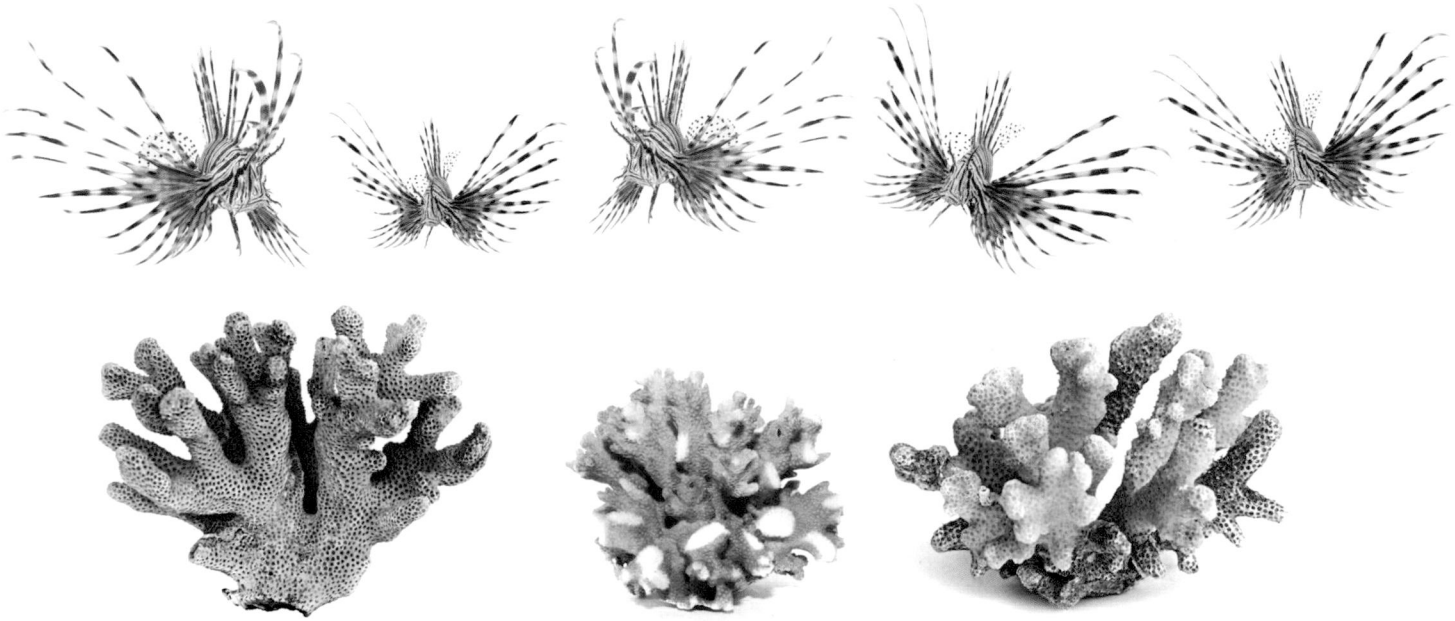

Matching pair

Look at the six tall, slender giraffes. Can you spot two that are exactly the same?

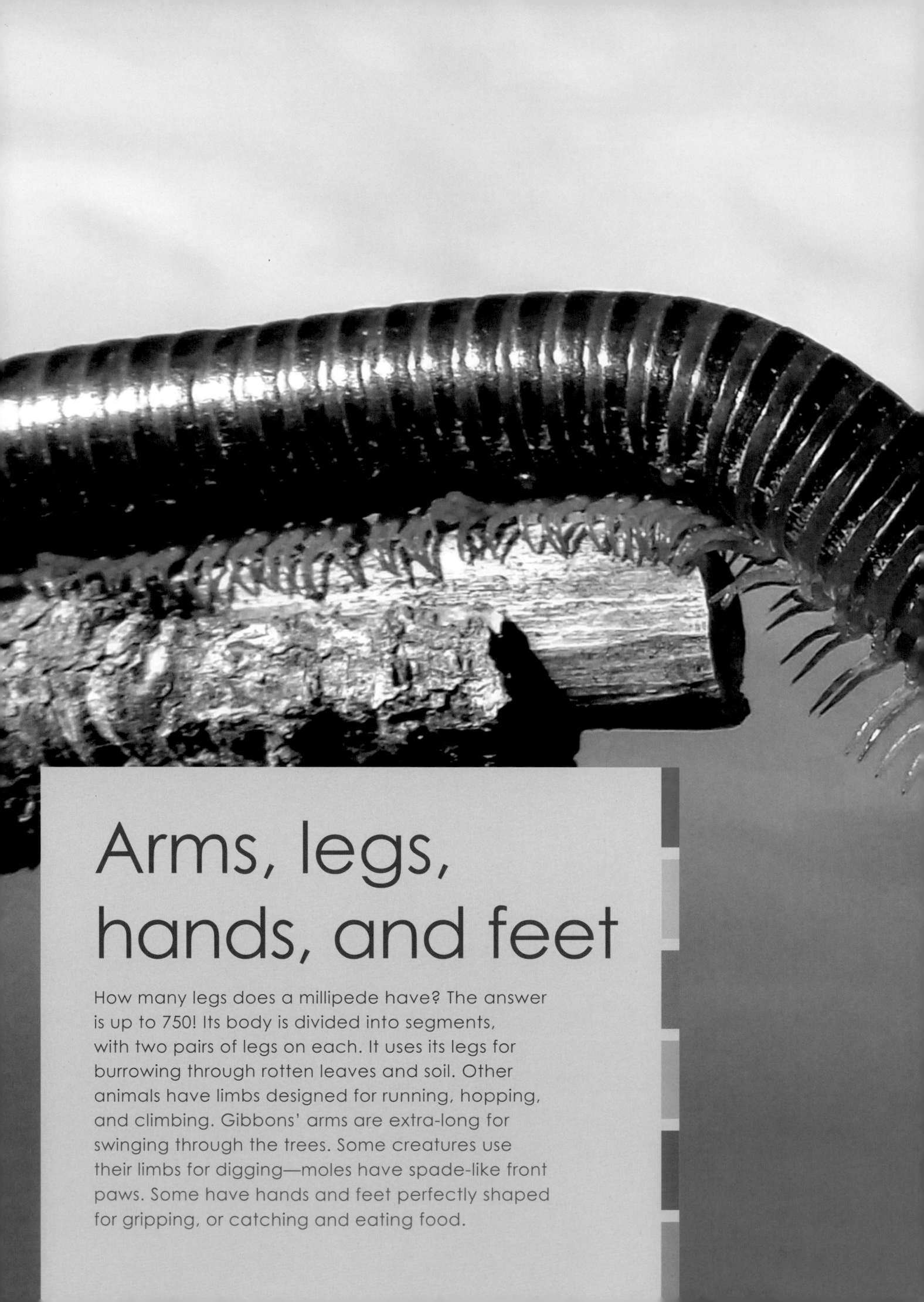

Arms, legs, hands, and feet

How many legs does a millipede have? The answer is up to 750! Its body is divided into segments, with two pairs of legs on each. It uses its legs for burrowing through rotten leaves and soil. Other animals have limbs designed for running, hopping, and climbing. Gibbons' arms are extra-long for swinging through the trees. Some creatures use their limbs for digging—moles have spade-like front paws. Some have hands and feet perfectly shaped for gripping, or catching and eating food.

Malu millipedes
Bonobo
Gibbon
Mouse
Orangutan
Bengal cats
Lion
Poison dart frogs
Greater Egyptian jerboa
Basset hound
Huntsman spiders
Great Dane
Tree frog
Foals
Scorpion

Orangutan
Caterpillar
White-cheeked gibbon
Caique
Andalusian horse
Brown bear
Grey heron
Secretary birds
Kangaroo
Octopuses
Squirrel monkey
Crab spider
Somali wild donkey
Millipedes

Macaque
Brown spider monkey
Mantis
Orangutans
Centipedes
Capybara
Flamingos
California sea lions
Centipede
Gibbon
Tarantula
Otter
Cougar

Grasshopper
Lion cub
Chickens
Kitten
Flamingo
Sea star
Sea lion
Red-eyed tree frog
Stick insect
Brazilian galliwasp
Gambian pouched rat
Giraffe
Spurge hawk caterpillar
Prionus beetle
Jaguar
Raccoon
Blue-footed booby

Arms and legs

The animals in these puzzles use their arms and legs to bounce, crawl, run, and even swim!

Count the legs

Can you find two animals with eight legs?

STICKY FINGERS

The gecko uses its feet to grip onto smooth walls. It can even run upside-down across ceilings!

Follow the path

The kangaroo hops on its long back legs. Help it hop through the maze to find the baby.

start

finish

Sticker scene

Find the long-legged flamingoes on your sticker sheet. Put them into the lake to search for shrimp.

Use your stickers here!

Wings

Birds are kings of the air, with wings perfectly evolved for flight. A few birds have wings but cannot fly. Penguins use their wings to "fly" underwater instead. A bird's wings may be different shapes—long and slender for gliding, or short and pointed for speed. By flapping their wings incredibly fast, hummingbirds can hover in one place. Bats are flying mammals. Their wings are formed from their hands and arms. Their fingers are extra-long to support the leathery skin stretched across them. This dragonfly flutters through the air on beautifully colored wings.

Butterfly
Blue-tailed bee eater
European herring gull
Ring-necked parakeet
Rose chafer
Brahminy kite
Butterflies
Birds of paradise
Pigeon
Budgerigars
Owl butterfly
Common ravens

Atlas moths
Sea eagle
Rooster
Wasp
Roller bird
Macaw
Giant rhinoceros beetles
Hornbill
Hummingbird
Flying fish
Flies
Milkweed locust
Butterfly
Ladybug
Zebra finch
Stick insect
Eagle owl

Golden eagle
Goldfinches
Moths
Canada goose
Galapagos penguins
Hummingbird
Geese
Yellow bittern
Flying grasshopper
Bee eater
Bees
Parrot
Seagull

Barn owl
Peacock
Penguin
Alexandrine parakeet
Red palm weevils
Bats
Turkeys
Eastern pondhawk dragonfly

Wings

The skies are filled with flying creatures! Look for some fliers and flutterers in these puzzles.

Follow the lines

The goldfinches are after a juicy beetle. Which one will reach it?

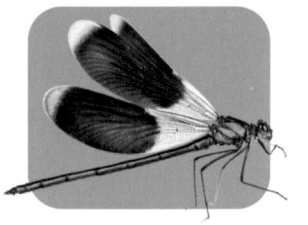

FURRY FLIER

The flying fox is the biggest bat in the world. Stretch your arms out to find out how big its wingspan is!

Spot the difference

Can you spot three differences between the two butterflies?

What comes next?

Look carefully at the winged animals. What comes next?
Use your stickers to fill in the gaps.

Use your stickers here!

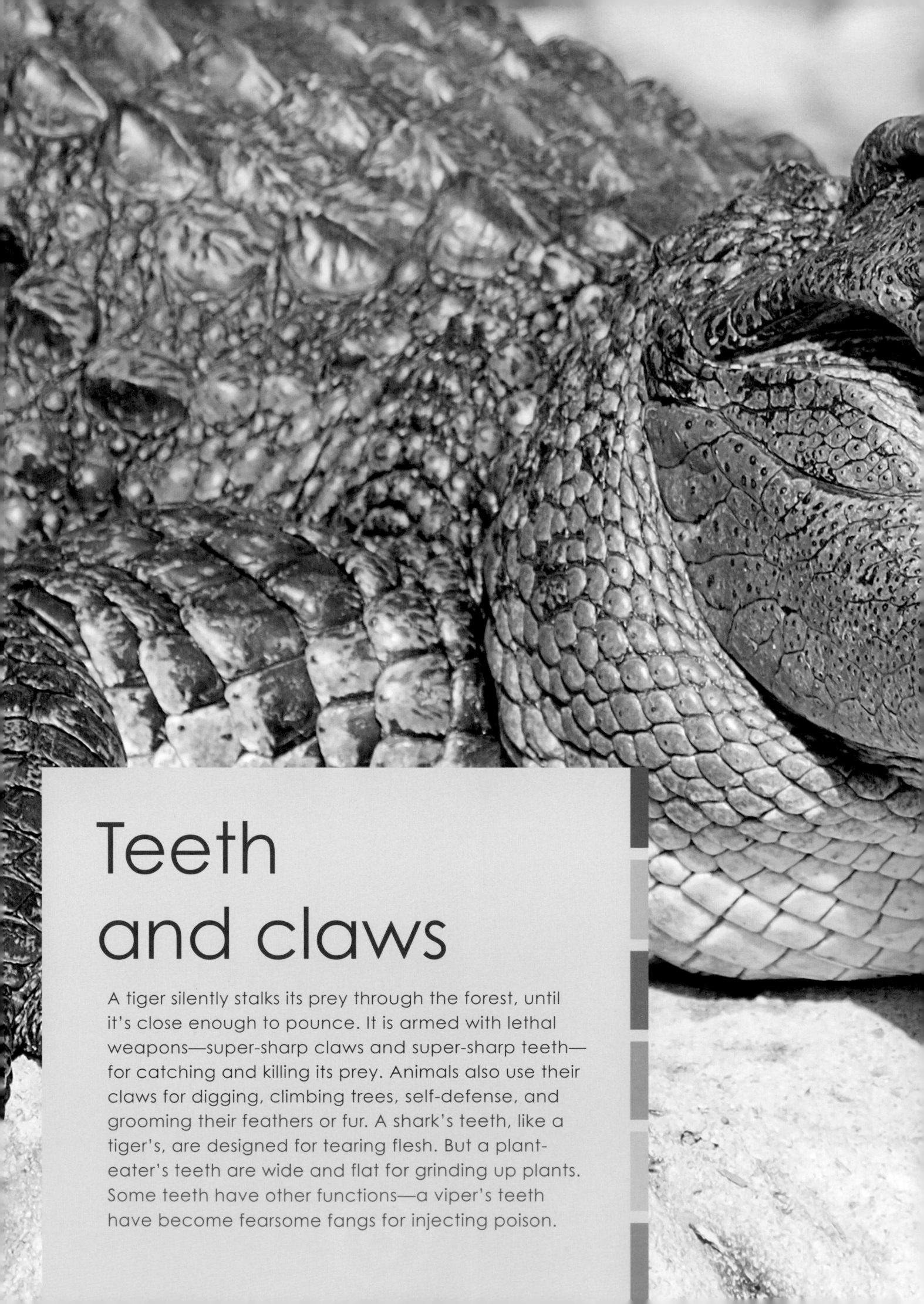

Teeth and claws

A tiger silently stalks its prey through the forest, until it's close enough to pounce. It is armed with lethal weapons—super-sharp claws and super-sharp teeth—for catching and killing its prey. Animals also use their claws for digging, climbing trees, self-defense, and grooming their feathers or fur. A shark's teeth, like a tiger's, are designed for tearing flesh. But a plant-eater's teeth are wide and flat for grinding up plants. Some teeth have other functions—a viper's teeth have become fearsome fangs for injecting poison.

Brown-patched kangaroo lizard
Blue crabs
Snake
Bluethroat bird
Scorpions
Prairie dog
North American beavers
Plumed basilisks
Cassowary
White tiger cub
American bald eagle
Crayfish
Crocodile
Tiger
Fiddler crab

Chick
Bat
Lion cubs
Eagle
Cat
Crocodile
Piranha fish
Brown bear
Wattled jacana birds
Hippopotamuses
Book scorpion

Eagle owl
Little owl
Polar bears
Lion
Lamprey fish
Collie
Skunk
Field crabs
Blue crayfish
African clawed frogs
Saarloos wolfdog
Spider crabs
Macaque

Two-toed sloth
Crayfish
British shorthair cat
Zebra
Hawk
Iguana
Panda
Horse
Small tufted deer

Razor-sharp teeth

Quick! Get your teeth into these puzzles before they start to snap, chomp, and bite!

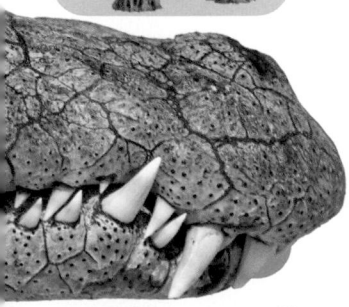

Shadow search

The sharp-toothed tiger shark is hunting. Look at the shadow. Which sea creatures has it found?

Squid

Turtle

Tuna

Crab

SUPER-TEETH!

Rabbits' teeth never stop growing! When the rabbits chew, it wears the teeth down and stops them getting too long.

Odd one out

Which snappy crocodile does not match the others?

Word search

Can you find these toothy animals in the word grid?

Mouse

b	d	p	n	s
e	l	i	o	n
a	m	g	t	a
r	w	l	b	k
m	o	u	s	e

Lion

Pig

Bear

Snake

Tearing claws

Animals use their sharp claws to grab things and to help them climb. Watch out for the claws in these puzzles!

Dot to dot

Connect the dots, starting with number 1. Which animal do the long claws belong to?

CLAWS OUT!

Tigers have extremely sharp, huge claws. Each claw is the length of your hand!

How many left?

The pandas use their claws to climb bamboo canes and eat the leaves. Are there enough leaves for all the pandas?

Sticker scene

Can you find the eagles on your sticker sheet? Add them to the scene.

Use your stickers here!

Glow in the dark

Some curious creatures, in the sea and on land, are able to make their own light—a wonder of the natural world. They may live in places, like the darkest depths of the sea, where there is little light, or only come out at dusk. They use their lights to attract prey, camouflage themselves, frighten attackers, or send signals. Glow-worms flash their lights in the darkness to attract mates. Each species has its own pattern of flashes that allows individuals to recognize each other. These jellyfish create their own light using a process called "bioluminescence."

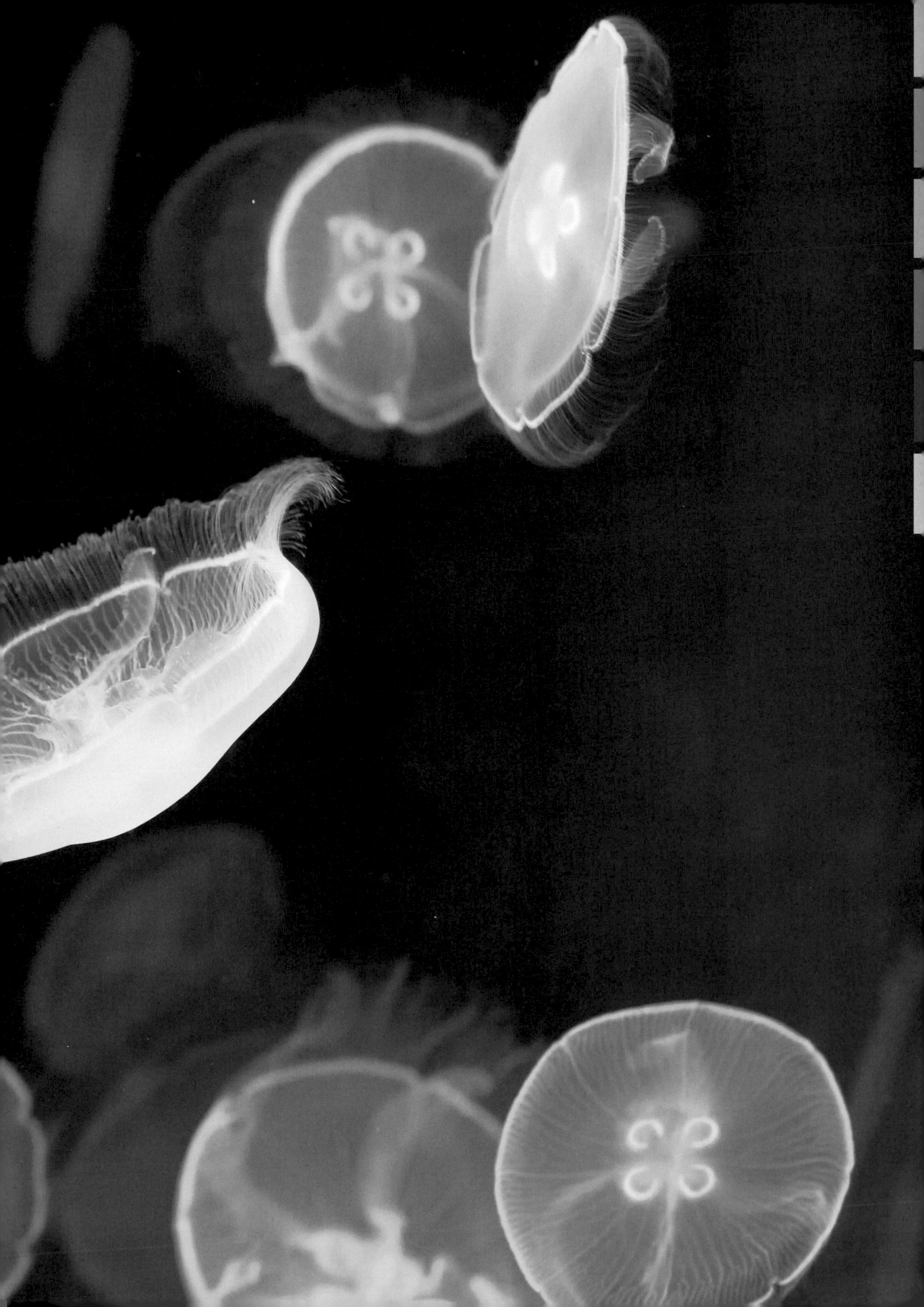

Fireflies
Jellyfish
Bioluminescent algae
Larval tube anemone

Comb jellyfish
Japanese sea nettle jellyfish
Sea slugs
Jellyfish
Filefish

Glowworm
Crystal jellyfish
Bioluminescent mushrooms
Moon jellyfish
Click beetle
Bioluminescent scorpion
Copepods
Comb jelly

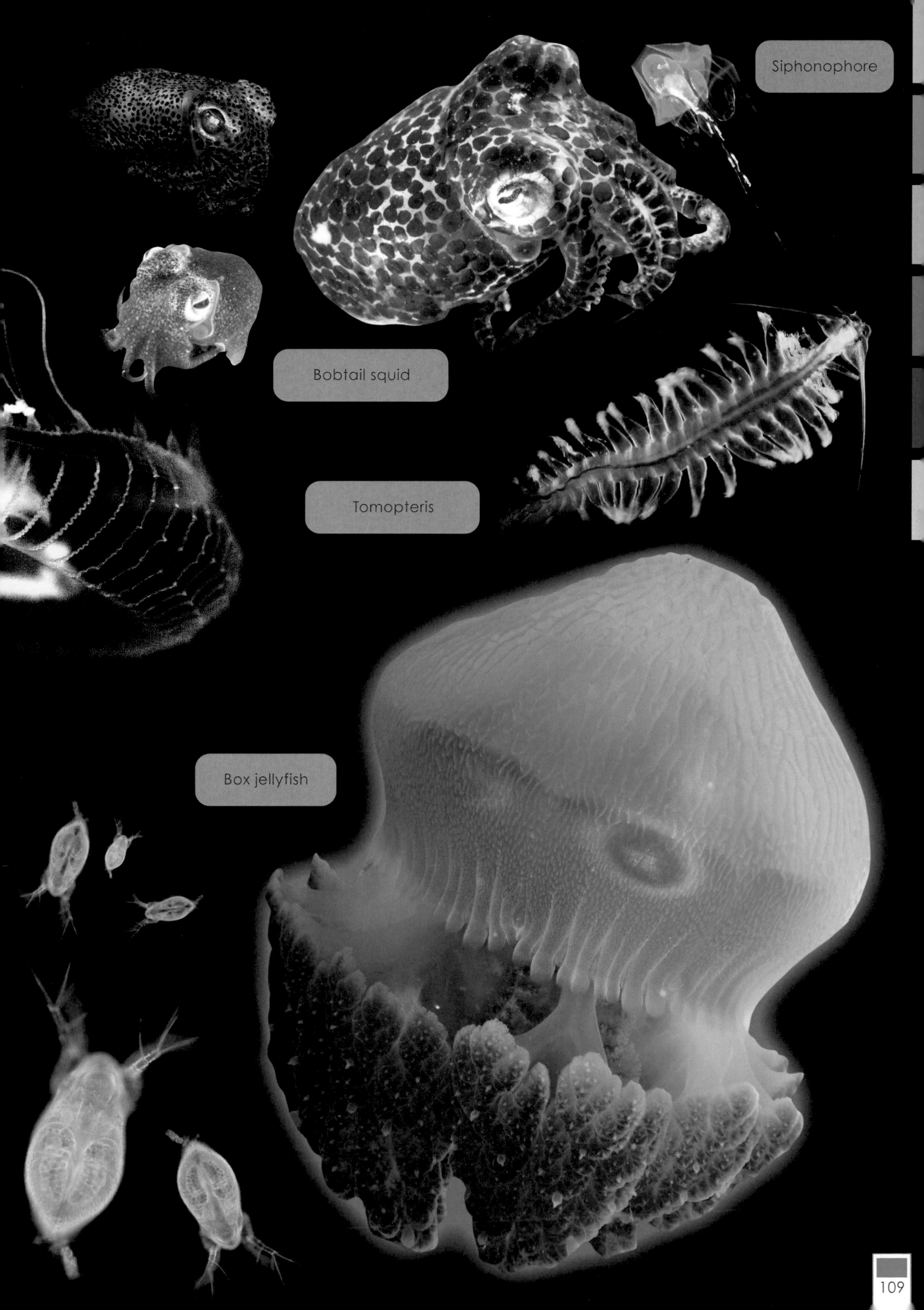
Siphonophore
Bobtail squid
Tomopteris
Box jellyfish

Glow in the dark

Some animals can make their own light. They shine and flash to send messages to each other.

Matching pair

Look at the twinkling jellyfish. Can you find a matching pair?

LIGHT SHOW

The blue-ringed octopus makes flashing patterns with its lights. It uses its flashes to warn predators to go away.

Maze

The flashing squid is trying to find its friends. Can you help it?

Follow the lines

The glowing fireflies are flying towards lights. Which one will reach its friend?